HAMMOND
my first atlas

Illustrated by
Gary Hincks and Nicki Palin

Written by
Nicholas Harris

Mapmakers for the 21st Century

CONTENTS

THE WORLD

THE WORLD is round. So, to make a map of the world appear on a flat page, the world's curved surface must be flattened out and parts of it stretched. The world map *(below)* is the result. The maps in this atlas show different areas of the world. Look for the little world map printed on each page. The part shaded red shows where in the world that area is situated.

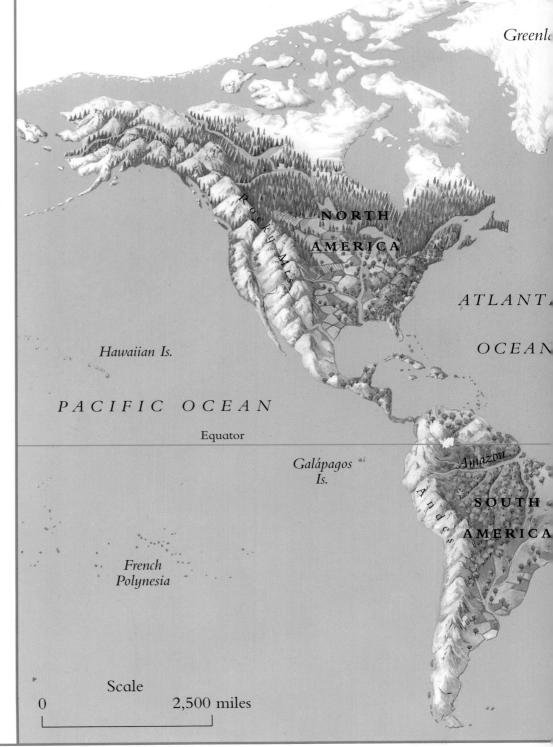

HOW TO USE THIS ATLAS

The maps in this atlas have been specially drawn to show where different kinds of landscape are found.

Arctic lands (tundra)

Mountains

Desert

Forest and woodlands

Coniferous forest

Farmland

Grassland

Marshes

Rivers and lakes

A scale bar *(below)* tells us how far distances on the map are in the real world. You can use it to work out longer or shorter distances.

Scale

0   100 miles

Boundaries between countries are shown in this atlas by red lines *(below left)*. Boundaries between states within countries, or disputed boundaries, are both shown by broken lines *(below right)*.

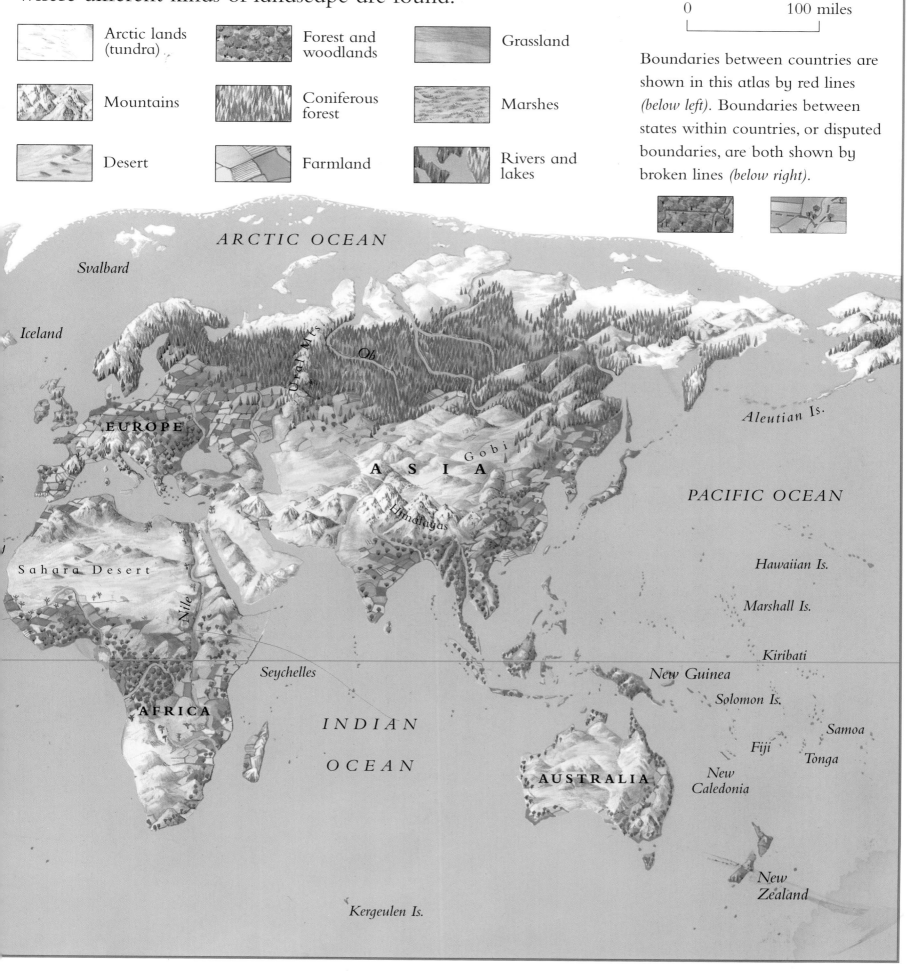

ARCTIC OCEAN

Svalbard

Iceland

Ural Mts.

Ob

EUROPE

ASIA

Gobi

Aleutian Is.

PACIFIC OCEAN

Himalayas

Sahara Desert

Nile

Hawaiian Is.

Marshall Is.

Kiribati

Seychelles

New Guinea

Solomon Is.

AFRICA

INDIAN

OCEAN

AUSTRALIA

Samoa

Fiji

Tonga

New Caledonia

New Zealand

Kergeulen Is.

Killer whales swim in the Arctic seas.

This pipeline carries oil across Alaska. It is built above the ground so that caribou can pass underneath it.

DID YOU KNOW . . ?

Canada has two languages, English and French. The French were the first Europeans to settle Canada but the British won control after a war. French is still spoken in the province of Québec, English elsewhere.

For many years, the native peoples of Canada's western coast carved totem poles. The poles stand at the doorways of their village homes. The wood carvings show figures and animals that were important in the history of their families.

ALASKA
(US)

Yukon

ANCHORAGE

PACIFIC OCEAN

YUKON TERRITORY

Rocky Mountains

Mackenzie

ARCTIC OCEAN

Banks Island

Victoria Island

Ellesmere Island

Great Bear Lake

NORTHWEST TERRITORIES

NUNAVUT

Great Slave Lake

C A N A D A

BRITISH COLUMBIA

ALBERTA

EDMONTON

MANITOBA

SASKATCHEWAN

Saskatchewan

VANCOUVER

CALGARY

REGINA

WINNIPEG

CANADA AND THE ARCTIC

CANADA is the second largest country in the world, after Russia. The northern region of Canada, known as tundra, is a frozen wasteland for about nine months of the year. Further south lie vast coniferous forests. Rising in the west are the craggy Rocky and Coast Mountains. Nearly all of Canada's cities lie close to the border with the USA and in the fertile grasslands known as the prairies. Alaska, a state of the USA, is a land of tundra and forests.

GREENLAND
(Denmark)

BAFFIN BAY

Baffin Island

HUDSON BAY

ATLANTIC OCEAN

NEWFOUNDLAND

QUÉBEC

St. Lawrence

ONTARIO

Lake Superior

QUÉBEC

MONTRÉAL

Lake Huron

NEW BRUNSWICK

PR. EDWARD I.

NOVA SCOTIA

TORONTO L. Ontario

Scale

0   400 miles

L. Erie

The Canadian Pacific Railway was completed more than 100 years ago. It links Canada's eastern and western coasts. Here, it crosses the spectacular Rocky Mountains. The trains mostly carry cargo, although the route is also popular with tourists.

The Inuit live in northern Canada and Greenland. Many Inuit still hunt whales, seals and caribou. Nowadays they use modern equipment such as snowmobiles and rifles.

UNITED STATES OF AMERICA

THE United States of America stretches from Atlantic to Pacific coasts of North America. The eastern USA is made up of the wooded Appalachian Mountains and fertile plains. The center of the country, the Mississippi lowlands, is mainly farmland. In the west, the landscape is mountainous. Here the climate, apart from on the Pacific coast, is much drier.

Once settled only by Native Americans, the USA is now home to people who came from all over the world to live here.

Scale

0   300 miles

SEATTLE

WASHINGTON

OREGON

MONTANA

IDAHO

ROCKY MTS

WYOMING

Snake

SALT LAKE CITY

NEVADA

UTAH

DENVER

PACIFIC OCEAN

SAN FRANCISCO

COLORADO

Colorado

CALIFORNIA

LOS ANGELES

ARIZONA

NEW MEXICO

PHOENIX

Rio

Baseball is a popular summer sport in the USA. It is played between two teams of nine players on a diamond-shaped field. Batters attempt to strike a ball thrown towards them by a pitcher.

The centers of many American cities are often crowded with skyscrapers. Seattle, in the northwest, also has the Space Needle. From the top there is a superb view of the city and the mountains nearby.

HONOLULU

HAWAII

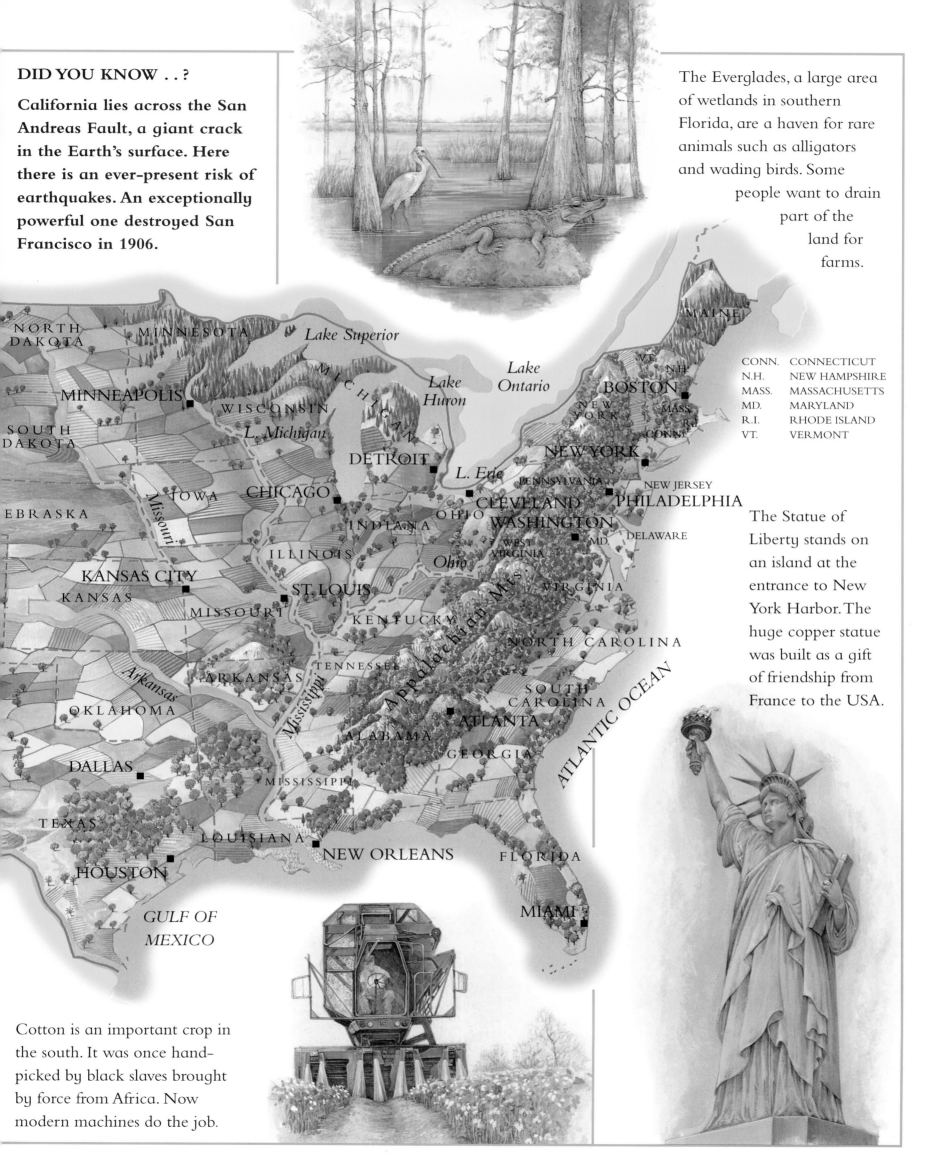

California lies across the San Andreas Fault, a giant crack in the Earth's surface. Here there is an ever-present risk of earthquakes. An exceptionally powerful one destroyed San Francisco in 1906.

The Everglades, a large area of wetlands in southern Florida, are a haven for rare animals such as alligators and wading birds. Some people want to drain part of the land for farms.

CONN.	CONNECTICUT
N.H.	NEW HAMPSHIRE
MASS.	MASSACHUSETTS
MD.	MARYLAND
R.I.	RHODE ISLAND
VT.	VERMONT

The Statue of Liberty stands on an island at the entrance to New York Harbor. The huge copper statue was built as a gift of friendship from France to the USA.

NORTH DAKOTA
MINNESOTA
Lake Superior
MAINE
Lake Ontario
VT.
N.H.
BOSTON
NEW YORK
MASS.
CONN.
R.I.
MINNEAPOLIS
WISCONSIN
MICHIGAN
Lake Huron
L. Michigan
SOUTH DAKOTA
L. Michigan
DETROIT
L. Erie
NEW YORK
EBRASKA
IOWA
Missouri
CHICAGO
PENNSYLVANIA
NEW JERSEY
PHILADELPHIA
INDIANA
OHIO
CLEVELAND
WASHINGTON
ILLINOIS
Ohio
WEST VIRGINIA
MD.
DELAWARE
KANSAS CITY
ST. LOUIS
VIRGINIA
KANSAS
MISSOURI
KENTUCKY
NORTH CAROLINA
Arkansas
ARKANSAS
TENNESSEE
Appalachian Mts.
OKLAHOMA
Mississippi
SOUTH CAROLINA
ATLANTIC OCEAN
DALLAS
ALABAMA
ATLANTA
GEORGIA
TEXAS
MISSISSIPPI
LOUISIANA
HOUSTON
NEW ORLEANS
FLORIDA
GULF OF MEXICO
MIAMI

Cotton is an important crop in the south. It was once hand-picked by black slaves brought by force from Africa. Now modern machines do the job.

Much of northern Mexico is covered by desert. The cactus is often the only plant life here.

MEXICALI

Sierra Madre

GULF OF CALIFORNIA

Scale
0   250 miles

Río Grande

MONTERREY

M E X I C O

GULF OF MEXICO

GUADALAJARA

MEXICO CITY

MÉRID

In many Central American and Caribbean countries, growing bananas is the most important industry. As the bananas grow, workers cover them with bags to protect them from insects. The bananas are cut down while they are still green. They ripen just before they go on sale.

BELIZ

GUATEMALA

EL SALVADO

PACIFIC OCEAN

The Panama Canal links the Atlantic and Pacific Oceans. Before the canal was built, ships had to go around in the stormy seas off the southern tip of South America. A series of locks were built to take canal traffic across the 50-mile stretch of land. Small trains help pull the ships through the locks.

8

Hand weaving is an ancient Indian art that still goes on in Mexico and Guatemala. Each region has its own style.

MEXICO AND CENTRAL AMERICA

MEXICO and the Central American countries stretch from the United States in the north to South America in the south. A mountain chain runs all the way down. There are many active volcanoes and the land is regularly shaken by earthquakes too. In the north the climate is dry, but further south there is tropical rainforest.

The Caribbean islands have a tropical climate. They often suffer fierce hurricanes.

BAHAMAS

HAVANA

TURKS & CAICOS IS. (Br.)

ANGUILLA (Br.)

VIRGIN IS. (Br. & US)

ANTIGUA

CUBA

ST. KITTS & NEVIS

GUADELOUPE (Fr.)

HAITI

DOMINICAN REPUBLIC

PUERTO RICO (US)

DOMINICA

MARTINIQUE (Fr.)

ST. LUCIA

BARBADOS

JAMAICA

ST. VINCENT AND THE GRENADINES

GRENADA

CARIBBEAN SEA

NETHERLANDS ANTILLES

TRINIDAD AND TOBAGO

NDURAS

ARAGUA

Panama Canal

COSTA RICA

PANAMA

Steel band music is popular on every Caribbean island. It was first played in Trinidad. The pans or drums are made from large oil drums. Calypso and Reggae music both have their origins in the Caribbean.

SOUTH AMERICA

THE CLIMATE in the northern part of South America is hot and rainy. The great Amazon Rainforest fills the Amazon River basin, a vast lowland area lying between the Andes and the Brazilian Highlands. The Andes mountains stretch all the way down the western edge of the continent to its cold, stormy southern tip, Cape Horn. Most of South America's farmland and cities are in the east, in southeastern Brazil and northern Argentina.

DID YOU KNOW . . ?

The Amazon River is about 4,000 miles long. It carries more water than any other river—more than the world's eight longest rivers put together.

These Indians take home their catch—an anaconda.

CARACAS ■
VENEZUELA
Orinoco
BOGOTÁ ■
COLOMBIA
GUYANA
SURINAME
FRENCH
GUIANA
QUITO ■
ECUADOR
Negro
Amazon
Amazon Rainforest
BRAZIL
Madeira
PERU
LIMA ■
L. Titicaca
BOLIVIA
LA PAZ ■
Brazilian Highlands
RECIFE ■

PACIFIC OCEAN

Scale
0   350 miles

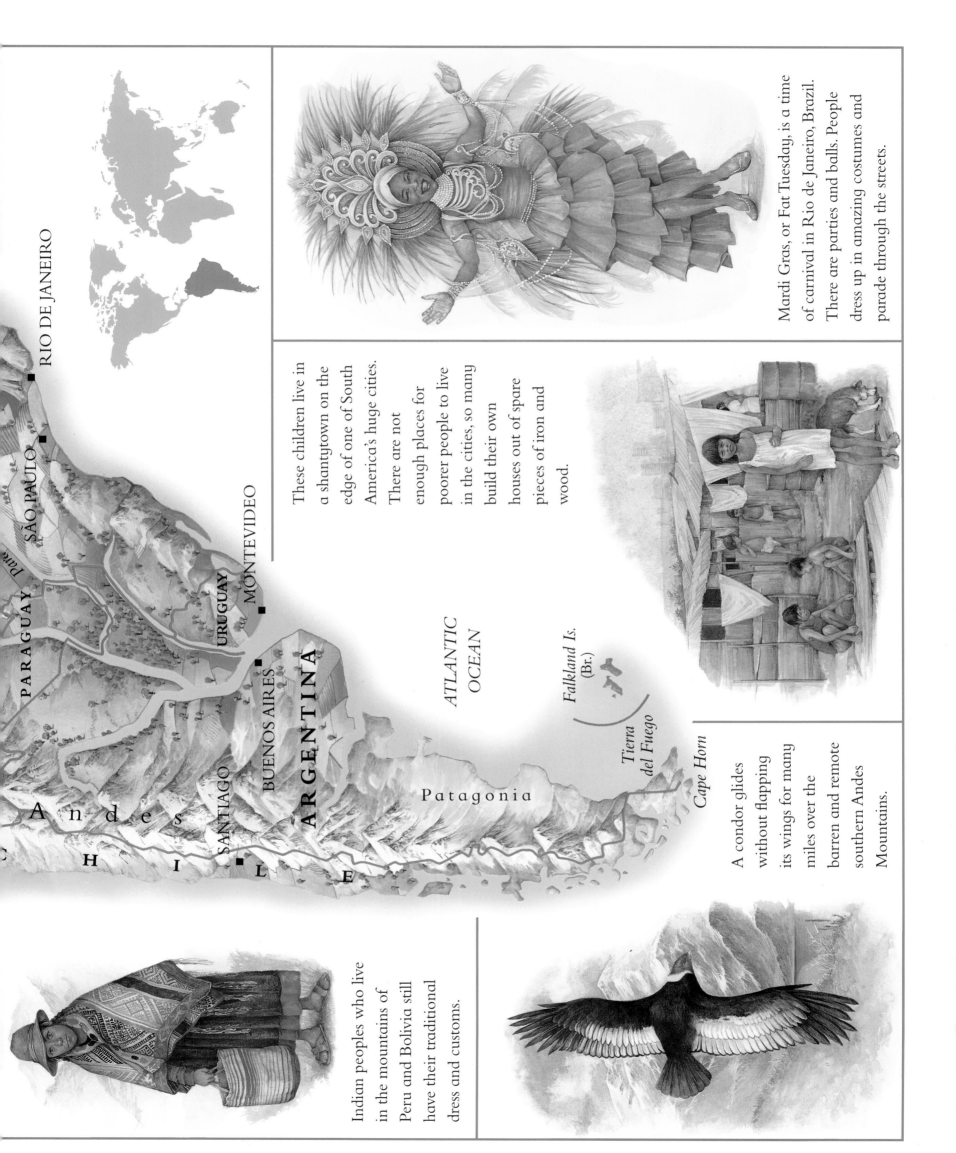

RIO DE JANEIRO

Mardi Gras, or Fat Tuesday, is a time of carnival in Rio de Janeiro, Brazil. There are parties and balls. People dress up in amazing costumes and parade through the streets.

SÃO PAULO

PARAGUAY

URUGUAY

MONTEVIDEO

BUENOS AIRES

ARGENTINA

SANTIAGO

A n d e s

C   H   I   L   E

Patagonia

ATLANTIC OCEAN

Falkland Is. (Br.)

Tierra del Fuego

Cape Horn

These children live in a shantytown on the edge of one of South America's huge cities. There are not enough places for poorer people to live in the cities, so many build their own houses out of spare pieces of iron and wood.

Indian peoples who live in the mountains of Peru and Bolivia still have their traditional dress and customs.

A condor glides without flapping its wings for many miles over the barren and remote southern Andes Mountains.

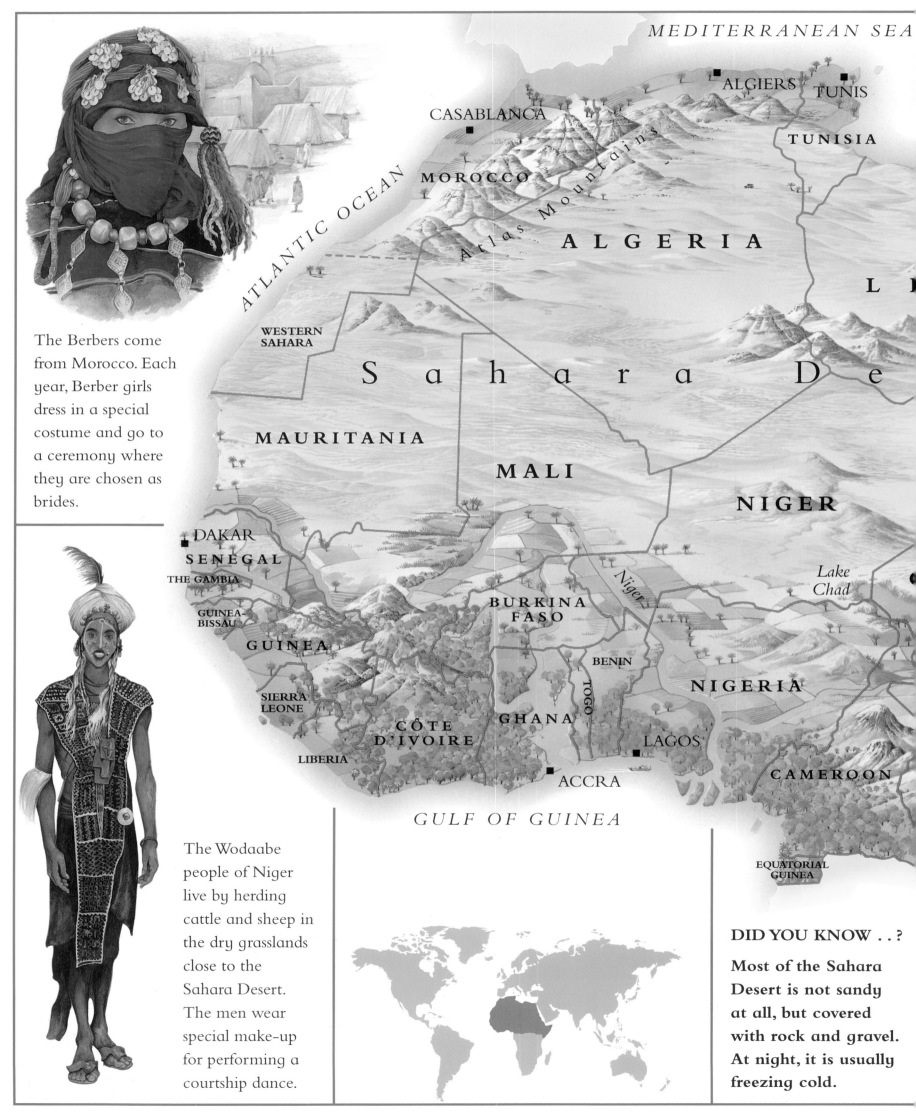

The Berbers come from Morocco. Each year, Berber girls dress in a special costume and go to a ceremony where they are chosen as brides.

The Wodaabe people of Niger live by herding cattle and sheep in the dry grasslands close to the Sahara Desert. The men wear special make-up for performing a courtship dance.

MEDITERRANEAN SEA

ATLANTIC OCEAN

CASABLANCA
ALGIERS
TUNIS
TUNISIA
MOROCCO
Atlas Mountains
ALGERIA
L
WESTERN SAHARA
Sahara De
MAURITANIA
MALI
NIGER
DAKAR
SENEGAL
THE GAMBIA
Niger
Lake Chad
GUINEA-BISSAU
BURKINA FASO
GUINEA
BENIN
NIGERIA
SIERRA LEONE
TOGO
CÔTE D'IVOIRE
GHANA
LAGOS
LIBERIA
ACCRA
CAMEROON

GULF OF GUINEA

EQUATORIAL GUINEA

DID YOU KNOW . . ?

Most of the Sahara Desert is not sandy at all, but covered with rock and gravel. At night, it is usually freezing cold.

I MOM dad I LUV YOU and I LUV OLSO I like you DOG Z and cats and I LUV DOG

LUV Leon craze girl

The ancient Egyptian pyramids are about 4,500 years old.

NORTHERN AFRICA

THE SAHARA is the largest hot desert in the world. It stretches right across North Africa, from the Atlantic Ocean to the Red Sea. The only river that runs across it is the Nile, the world's longest river. The Nile has farmland close to its banks.

If you travel south from the Sahara, you will come across grassy plains. Near the West African coast there is some thick rainforest, although many trees have been cut down to make more room for farmland.

Y A
r t

EGYPT

CAIRO

RED SEA

Nile

KHARTOUM

ERITREA

A D

S U D A N

DJIBOUTI

ADDIS ABABA

CENTRAL AFRICAN REPUBLIC

E T H I O P I A

S O M A L I A

Scale
0   500 miles

The Sahara is a vast, dry desert. But there are some places where water can be found. These are called oases.

This is a fruit market in West Africa. People carrying containers around on their heads are a common sight.

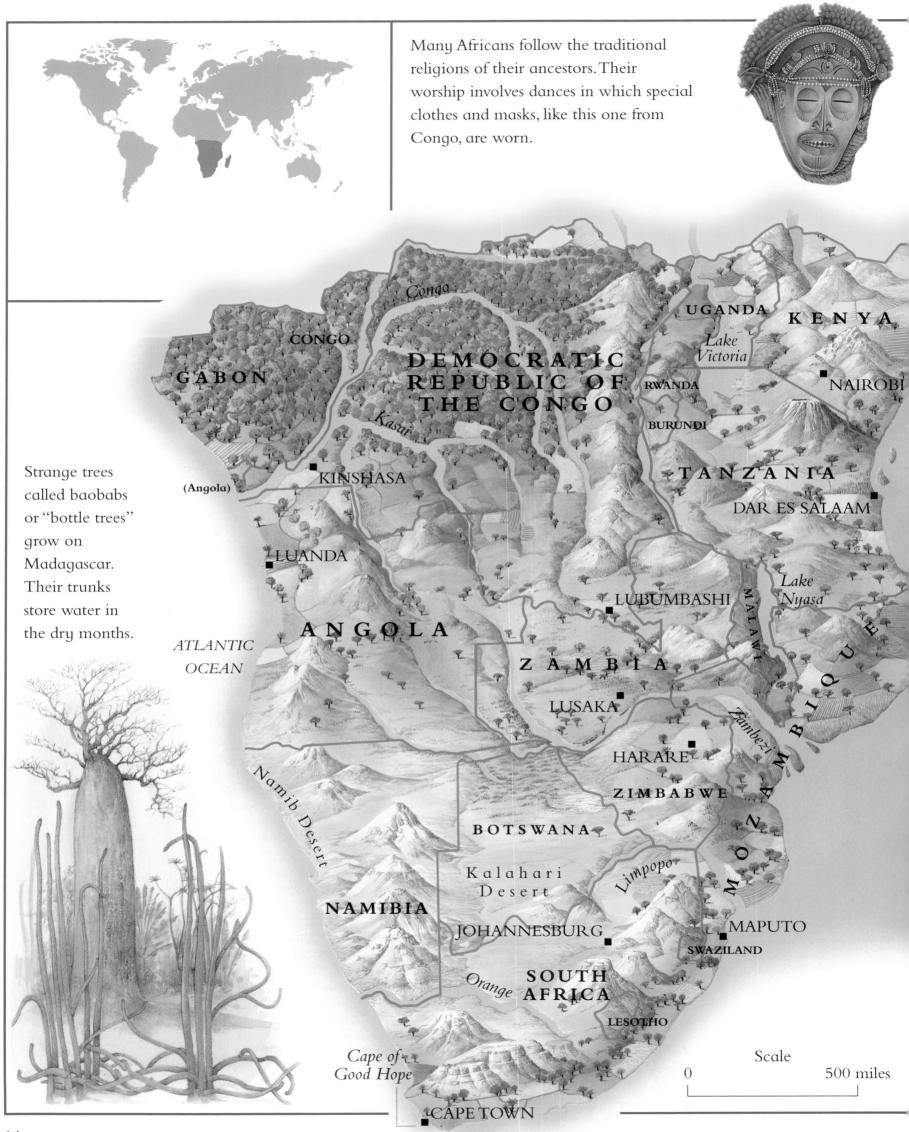

Many Africans follow the traditional religions of their ancestors. Their worship involves dances in which special clothes and masks, like this one from Congo, are worn.

Strange trees called baobabs or "bottle trees" grow on Madagascar. Their trunks store water in the dry months.

CONGO

GABON

DEMOCRATIC REPUBLIC OF THE CONGO

Congo

Kasai

(Angola)

KINSHASA

UGANDA

KENYA

Lake Victoria

RWANDA

NAIROBI

BURUNDI

TANZANIA

DAR ES SALAAM

LUANDA

Lake Nyasa

LUBUMBASHI

ANGOLA

ATLANTIC OCEAN

ZAMBIA

MALAWI

LUSAKA

Zambezi

HARARE

ZIMBABWE

MOZAMBIQUE

Namib Desert

BOTSWANA

Limpopo

K a l a h a r i D e s e r t

NAMIBIA

JOHANNESBURG

MAPUTO

SWAZILAND

Orange SOUTH AFRICA

LESOTHO

Cape of Good Hope

Scale

0   500 miles

CAPE TOWN

The Maasai people come from East Africa, where they herd cattle. They wear the same beautiful ornaments that their ancestors did centuries ago. Girls older than nine adorn themselves with colorful necklaces and fantastic earrings.

SOUTHERN AFRICA

THE SOUTHERN half of Africa also has deserts: the Kalahari and the Namib in the southwest. But most of the region is covered either by rainforest, in the Congo Basin, or dry grasslands. The Great Rift Valley, a long "crack" in the Earth's surface, runs down through East Africa, a region of mountains, volcanoes and long lakes.

Africa is famous for the huge variety of animals that roam across its plains. Giraffes, wildebeests, elephants, zebras and rhinoceroses live here, along with predators such as lions, cheetahs and hyenas.

Many countries of Southern Africa are rich in copper, diamonds, gold and other minerals. Miners drill the rock deep below the surface. Many local people are employed in the mines.

INDIAN OCEAN

COMOROS

NTANANARIVO

ADAGASCAR

DID YOU KNOW . . ?

Thousands of tourists visit Africa's wildlife parks, where the animals are protected by law. Unfortunately, many animals, such as elephants and rhinos, are killed by poachers, who then cut off and sell their tusks and horns. Some animals are now endangered.

Savannah, dry grassland with open woodland, covers the East African plains. Herds of animals, such as giraffes and zebras, live here.

WESTERN EUROPE

THE WESTERN lands of Europe stretch from the windy, wet Shetlands in the far north to the hot southern coasts of Spain and Portugal. The Atlantic Ocean brings cooling breezes in summer, but also mild weather in winter. The western coasts of the British Isles, Brittany and northwestern Spain have quite frequent rainfall. In the warmer, drier areas of France, Spain and Portugal, the climate is perfect for vineyards.

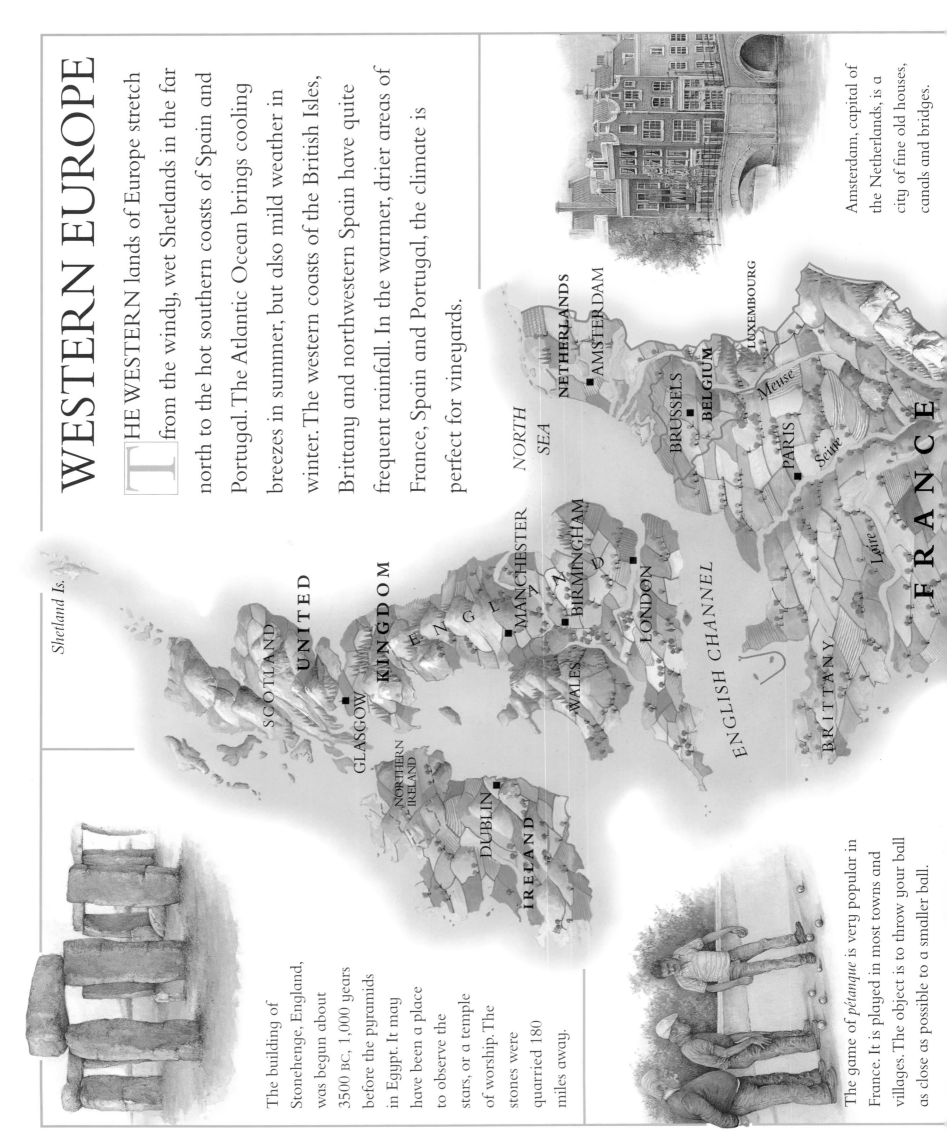

Shetland Is.

SCOTLAND

UNITED

GLASGOW

KINGDOM

NORTHERN IRELAND

ENGLAND

MANCHESTER

BIRMINGHAM

WALES

LONDON

DUBLIN

IRELAND

ENGLISH CHANNEL

BRITTANY

NORTH SEA

NETHERLANDS

AMSTERDAM

BELGIUM

BRUSSELS

LUXEMBOURG

Meuse

PARIS

Seine

FRANCE

Loire

Amsterdam, capital of the Netherlands, is a city of fine old houses, canals and bridges.

The building of Stonehenge, England, was begun about 3500 BC, 1,000 years before the pyramids in Egypt. It may have been a place to observe the stars, or a temple of worship. The stones were quarried 180 miles away.

The game of *pétanque* is very popular in France. It is played in most towns and villages. The object is to throw your ball as close as possible to a smaller ball.

16

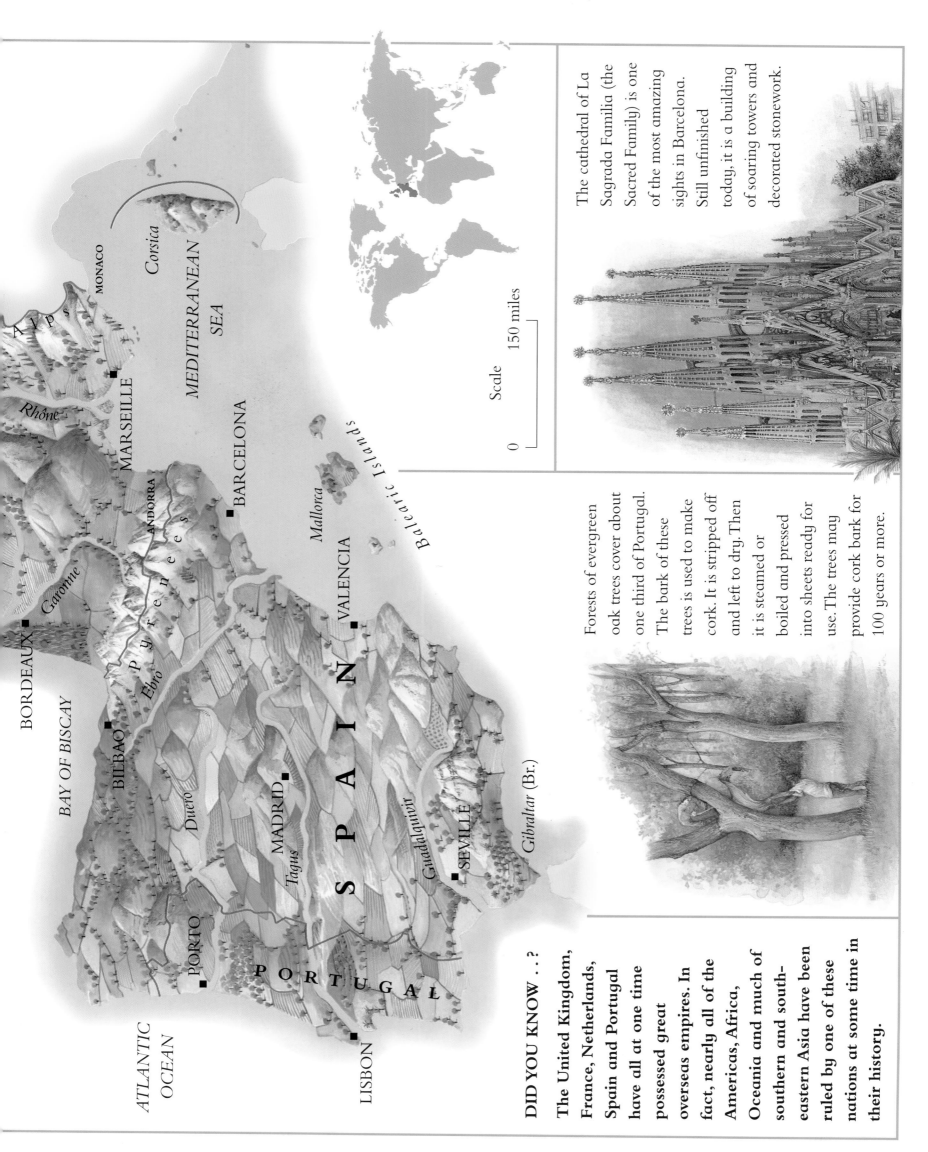

ATLANTIC
OCEAN

BAY OF BISCAY

Alps

Rhône

MONACO

Corsica

MEDITERRANEAN
SEA

MARSEILLE

Garonne

P y r e n e e s

ANDORRA

BARCELONA

BORDEAUX

BILBAO

Ebro

Mallorca

Balearic Islands

VALENCIA

Duero

S   P   A   I   N

MADRID

Tagus

Guadalquivir

SEVILLE

Gibraltar (Br.)

PORTO

P   O   R   T   U   G   A   L

LISBON

Scale

0   150 miles

The cathedral of La Sagrada Familia (the Sacred Family) is one of the most amazing sights in Barcelona. Still unfinished today, it is a building of soaring towers and decorated stonework.

Forests of evergreen oak trees cover about one third of Portugal. The bark of these trees is used to make cork. It is stripped off and left to dry. Then it is steamed or boiled and pressed into sheets ready for use. The trees may provide cork bark for 100 years or more.

DID YOU KNOW . . ?

The United Kingdom, France, Netherlands, Spain and Portugal have all at one time possessed great overseas empires. In fact, nearly all of the Americas, Africa, Oceania and much of southern and south-eastern Asia have been ruled by one of these nations at some time in their history.

SOUTHERN EUROPE

THE LANDS of southern Europe border the Mediterranean and Black Seas. Italy and Greece are made up of peninsulas and islands. Rivers such as the Danube and its tributaries, and the River Po in northern Italy, flow across wide fertile plains, but most of southern Europe is hilly or mountainous.

The ancient Greek civilization and the Roman Empire both began and spread across this region. Many historic remains still stand today.

The Parliament Building of Hungary stands on the eastern side of the River Danube in the capital, Budapest.

Building work began on the bell tower next to the Cathedral at Pisa, Italy, more than 800 years ago. Unfortunately, the ground beneath it was too soft and the tower began to lean. Today, engineers have made sure the Leaning Tower of Pisa will not fall over.

Marshes grow along the banks of the Danube near its mouth. Here, white pelicans come to nest in large numbers. They use their pouched bills to catch fish.

The ruins of buildings that were once magnificent temples are found all over Greece. This is Delphi, built on the slopes of Mount Parnassus. For the ancient Greeks, it was an important place of worship.

Southeast Europe is home to many different peoples and religions. This is a Muslim girl from Bosnia and Herzegovina.

DID YOU KNOW . . ?

The smallest country in the world is the Vatican City State. About one eighth the size of Central Park, in New York, it lies inside Rome, capital of Italy. The Vatican is the home of the Pope. It has its own newspaper, bank and railway station.

NORTHERN EUROPE

NORWAY, Sweden and Denmark are known as Scandinavia. Together with Finland, they are the most northerly European lands. Central Europe lies between the Baltic Sea and the Alps. The plains of northern Germany, Denmark and Poland are fertile. Evergreen forests cover upland areas, as well as low-lying Finland.

These sea inlets in Norway's coastline are called fjords.

Lapland is home to the Lapps, or Saami people. A few still herd reindeer, a traditional way of life.

Scale

150 miles

0

DID YOU KNOW . . ?
Northern Scandinavia is the Land of the Midnight Sun. At the height of summer, the sun never sets. But in the depths of winter, it never rises.

ICELAND
■ REYKJAVIK

LAPLAND

Inari

■ OULU

FINLAND

TALLINN
■

ESTONIA

GULF OF BOTHNIA

Åland

■ HELSINKI

■ STOCKHOLM

S W E D E N

Vänern

N O R W A Y

TRONDHEIM
■

BERGEN
■

OSLO
■

Mountains cover much of Austria and Switzerland. Many Austrian village churches have onion-shaped domes.

The River Rhine in Germany is a major waterway. Barges carry goods up and down it. They pass through the Rhine gorge, a land of castles and vine-covered slopes.

This man shapes a blob of melted glass by blowing into it. Glassblowing is a traditional industry of Poland.

LATVIA

LITHUANIA

VILNIUS
(RUSSIA)

BALTIC
SEA

DENMARK

COPENHAGEN

Bornholm

POLAND

WARSAW

Vistula

GDAŃSK

KRAKOW

SLOVAKIA

BRATISLAVA

BERLIN

HAMBURG

GERMANY

Elbe

PRAGUE

CZECH REPUBLIC

VIENNA

AUSTRIA

FRANKFURT

Danube

MUNICH

COLOGNE

Rhine

LIECHTENSTEIN

ZURICH

SWITZERLAND

A l p s

GENEVA

RUSSIA AND CENTRAL ASIA

R USSIA is the largest country in the world. It stretches across two continents, Europe and Asia. Most of its people live in the European part, to the west of the Ural Mountains. Siberia, the Asian part, is a land of mountains and forests. It is bitterly cold for much of the year.

This train travels on the Trans-Siberian Railway, the longest railway in the world. A trip from Moscow to Vladivostok takes eight days.

DID YOU KNOW . . ?

Lake Baikal is the deepest lake in the world. From surface to bottom, it is four times the height of the tallest skyscraper.

Novaya Zemlya

ST. PETERSBURG
L. Ladoga
ARKHANGELSK
MINSK
BELARUS
MOSCOW
KIEV
MOLDOVA
UKRAINE
KHARKOV
ROSTOV
Volga
R U S S I
Ural Mountains
YEKATERINBURG
Ob
SAMARA
Trans-Siberian Railway
OMSK
GEORGIA
KAZAKHSTAN
ARMENIA
(AZER-BAIJAN)
AZER-BAIJAN
Caspian Sea
Aral Sea
BAKU
UZBEKISTAN
Lake Balkhash
TURKMENISTAN
SAMARKAND
KYRGYZSTAN
TAJIKISTAN

This colorful building is St. Basil's Cathedral in Moscow, the capital city of Russia.

Scale
0   500 miles

ARCTIC
OCEAN

Lena

SIBERIA

Tunguska

Yenisei

*Kamchatka
Peninsula*

SEA OF
OKHOTSK

Sakhalin

Amur

Lake
Baikal

IRKUTSK

VLADIVOSTOK

Besides Russians, about 100 different peoples live in Russia. This Nenets woman lives in the Arctic region of Siberia.

The Siberian crane is 60 inches tall. The male bird sometimes performs a kind of dance.

This is the great gateway of an ancient Islamic building in Samarkand, a city in Uzbekistan.

23

Scale
0   300 miles

A whirling dervish from Turkey. A Muslim worshipper, he performs a special dance.

BLACK SEA

ISTANBUL

ANKARA

T U R K E Y

CASPIAN SEA

TABRIZ

CYPRUS

K U R D I S T A N

S Y R I A

TEHRAN

LEBANON

BEIRUT

I R A Q

I R A N

MEDITERRANEAN SEA

DAMASCUS

Tigris

BAGHDAD

DID YOU KNOW . . ?

The Kurds do not have a country of their own. Their land, Kurdistan, stretches across Turkey, Iraq and Iran.

JORDAN

Euphrates

JERUSALEM

ISRAEL

SHIRAZ

KUWAIT

P E R S I A N   G U L F

The Wailing Wall in Jerusalem is all that remains of an ancient Jewish temple. Many Jews go there to pray.

BAHRAIN

DUBAI

R E D   S E A

RIYADH

QATAR

S A U D I   A R A B I A

UNITED ARAB EMIRATES

JIDDAH

MECCA

Rub 'al Khali (Empty Quarter)

O M

SAN'A

Y E M E N

ARABIAN SEA

ADEN

THE MIDDLE EAST

SOUTHWESTERN ASIA is also known as the Middle East. Much of this region is very dry, although parts of the Mediterranean coast and the area lying between the Tigris and Euphrates rivers in Iraq are richly fertile. The world's earliest farming settlements grew up here. Turkey, Iran and Afghanistan are mountainous lands. Most of the Arabian Peninsula is desert.

MASHHAD

KABUL

AFGHANISTAN

MUSCAT

The Bedouin are nomads. They are a people who do not live in one place but wander with their animals across the desert lands of the Middle East.

The countries near the Persian Gulf have vast deposits of oil. It is transported to other countries around the world in tankers like this one.

The ancient city of San'a is the capital of Yemen. Lining its narrow, winding streets are these tall, carefully decorated houses. Built of stone and mud-brick with patterns made out of plaster, these early "skyscrapers" are hundreds of years old.

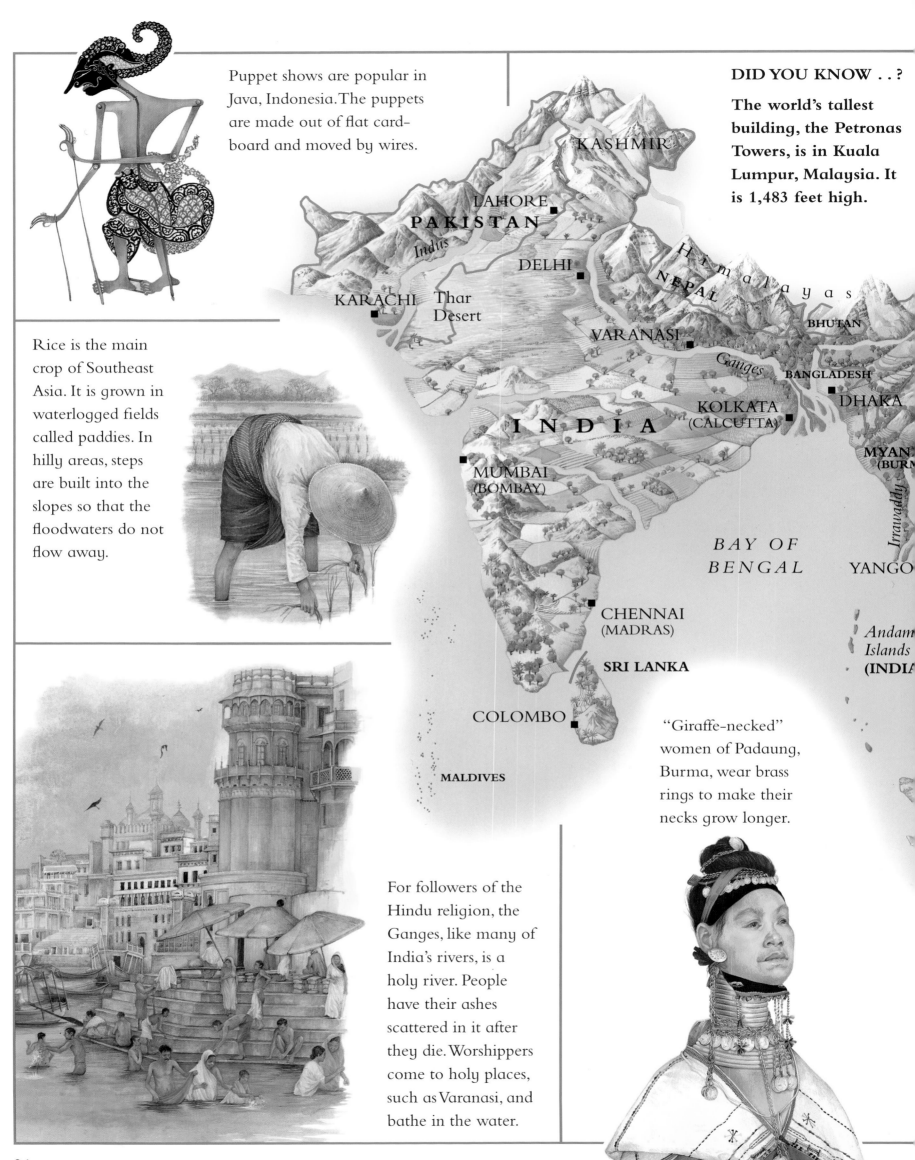

Puppet shows are popular in Java, Indonesia. The puppets are made out of flat cardboard and moved by wires.

DID YOU KNOW . . ?

The world's tallest building, the Petronas Towers, is in Kuala Lumpur, Malaysia. It is 1,483 feet high.

Rice is the main crop of Southeast Asia. It is grown in waterlogged fields called paddies. In hilly areas, steps are built into the slopes so that the floodwaters do not flow away.

KASHMIR

LAHORE

PAKISTAN

Indus

DELHI

NEPAL

KARACHI   Thar Desert

H i m a l a y a s

BHUTAN

VARANASI

Ganges

BANGLADESH

I N D I A

KOLKATA (CALCUTTA)

DHAKA

MYAN (BURM

MUMBAI (BOMBAY)

Irrawaddy

BAY OF BENGAL

YANGO

CHENNAI (MADRAS)

Andam Islands **(INDIA**

SRI LANKA

COLOMBO

"Giraffe-necked" women of Padaung, Burma, wear brass rings to make their necks grow longer.

MALDIVES

For followers of the Hindu religion, the Ganges, like many of India's rivers, is a holy river. People have their ashes scattered in it after they die. Worshippers come to holy places, such as Varanasi, and bathe in the water.

INDIA <small>AND</small> SOUTHEAST ASIA

INDIA has the world's second largest population after China. Most of its people live in the countryside. India's best farmland is found in the plains of the River Ganges. To the north lie the Himalayas, the world's highest mountains. Across the Thar Desert in the east is Pakistan, another country with a large population.

Travelling east, we reach the tropical rainforests of Southeast Asia. In many parts, the trees are being felled to make way for farmland, cities, reservoirs or quarries.

Elephants are still used in Thailand to clear forests and haul logs.

HANOI

LAOS

Mekong

SOUTH CHINA SEA

THAILAND

BANGKOK

CAMBODIA

VIETNAM

HO CHI MINH CITY

MANILA

PHILIPPINES

BRUNEI

KUALA LUMPUR

MALAYSIA

SINGAPORE

Borneo

Celebes

Moluccas

West Irian

Sumatra

INDONESIA

JAKARTA

INDIAN OCEAN

Java

Bali

Flores

EAST TIMOR

Scale

0

500 miles

CHINA AND JAPAN

CHINA has the largest population of any country in the world. About a fifth of the world's people live here. The mountains and deserts of the west are mostly empty. Eastern China has rich farmland and great cities. Japan is made up of four main islands. Thousands of earthquakes happen here every year.

DID YOU KNOW . . ?

The main language of China is Mandarin. There are many spoken versions, but only one kind of writing, which everyone can understand.

On some Chinese rivers, fishermen train cormorants to catch fish for them.

Takla Makan

M O

G

O

C

T I B E T

H i m a l a y a s

Salween

The Great Wall of China was built to stop raiders from the north invading China. The Wall is more than 1,800 miles long and is the largest structure ever built by people. It took many centuries to complete it.

In the Tibetan mountains, people live by herding yaks. This woman is churning yak's milk into butter.

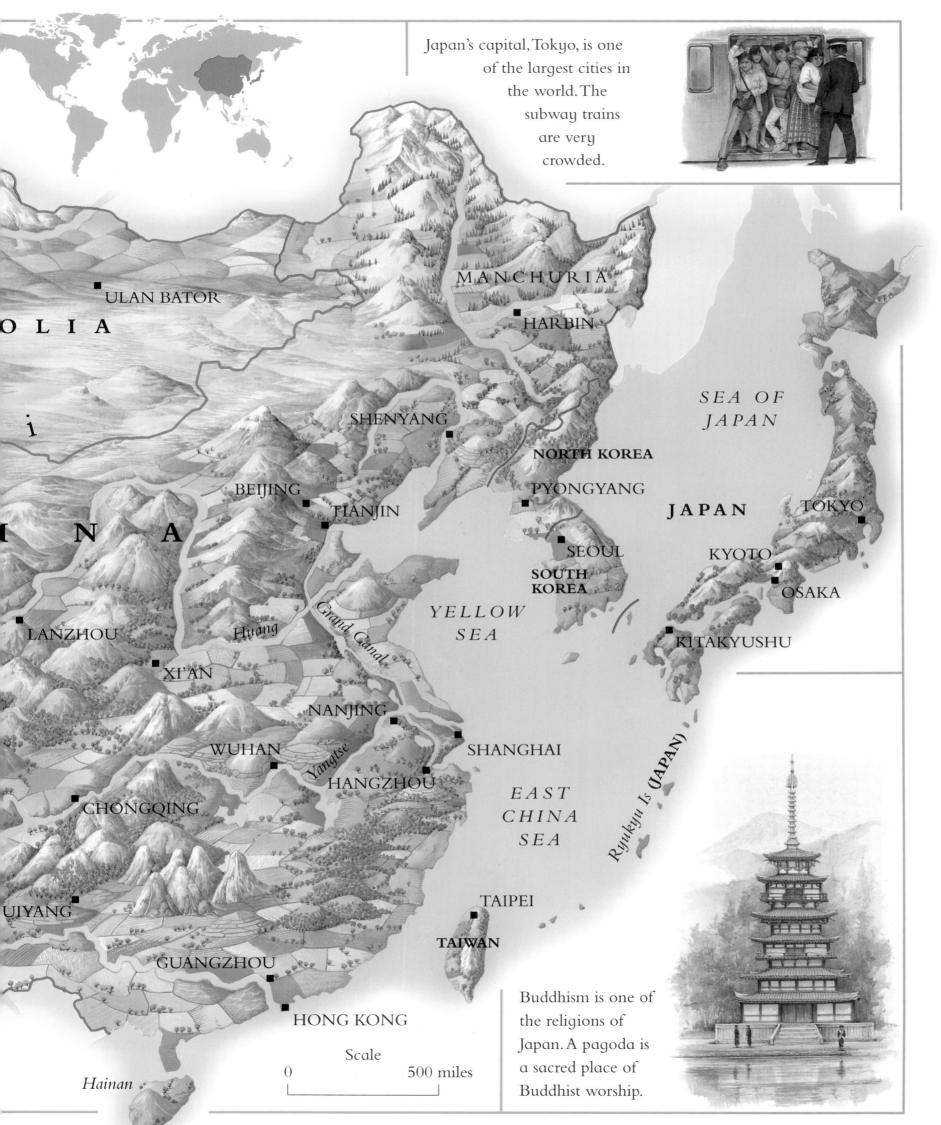

Japan's capital, Tokyo, is one of the largest cities in the world. The subway trains are very crowded.

ULAN BATOR

MANCHURIA

HARBIN

OLIA

i

SHENYANG

SEA OF
JAPAN

NORTH KOREA

BEIJING

PYONGYANG

JAPAN

TOKYO

TIANJIN

INA

SEOUL

KYOTO

SOUTH
KOREA

OSAKA

LANZHOU

Huang

YELLOW
SEA

Grand Canal

KITAKYUSHU

XI'AN

NANJING

WUHAN

Yangtse

SHANGHAI

HANGZHOU

EAST
CHINA
SEA

CHONGQING

Ryukyu Is (JAPAN)

UIYANG

TAIPEI

TAIWAN

GUANGZHOU

HONG KONG

Scale

0   500 miles

Hainan

Buddhism is one of the religions of Japan. A pagoda is a sacred place of Buddhist worship.

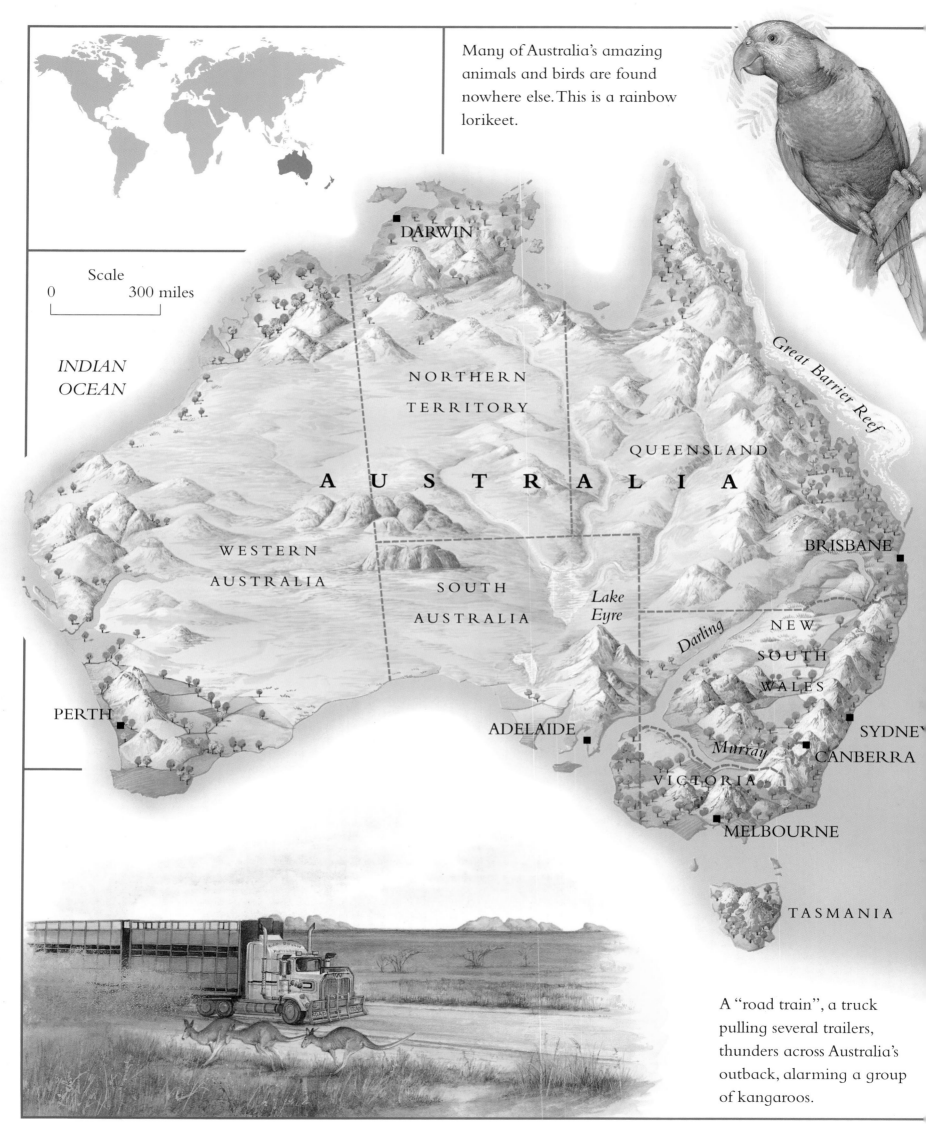

Many of Australia's amazing animals and birds are found nowhere else. This is a rainbow lorikeet.

Scale

0   300 miles

INDIAN OCEAN

DARWIN

NORTHERN TERRITORY

QUEENSLAND

Great Barrier Reef

A U S T R A L I A

WESTERN AUSTRALIA

SOUTH AUSTRALIA

BRISBANE

Lake Eyre

Darling

NEW SOUTH WALES

PERTH

ADELAIDE

Murray

SYDNEY

CANBERRA

VICTORIA

MELBOURNE

TASMANIA

A "road train", a truck pulling several trailers, thunders across Australia's outback, alarming a group of kangaroos.

Sydney, Australia's largest city, is built around a natural harbor. Its most famous landmarks are the Harbour Bridge and the "sail-roofed" Opera House.

Sheep farming is very important in both Australia and New Zealand. Together, they have more than 200 million sheep! Here, a shearer removes the fleece of a Merino sheep.

AUSTRALIA AND NEW ZEALAND

AUSTRALIA and New Zealand are part of Oceania. This region also includes Papua New Guinea and the islands of the Pacific Ocean (see pages 2-3).

Australia is large enough to be a continent itself. Nearly all its inhabitants live near the southeastern and south-western coasts. Here also are Australia's farmlands and vineyards. The rest of the country is almost empty. Most of the western and central regions, known as the outback, are dry grassland or desert.

New Zealand is made up of two large mountainous islands. Its warm, rainy climate is perfect for farming.

DID YOU KNOW . . ?

The Great Barrier Reef, just off Australia's northeast coast, is the world's largest living thing. More than 1,200 miles long, the reef is made of coral, the skeletons of tiny creatures. It is home to many kinds of fish.

AUCKLAND

North Island

TASMAN SEA

WELLINGTON

NEW ZEALAND

South Island

New Zealand was first inhabited by people only about 1,000 years ago. The first settlers were the Maoris. They were fierce warriors. Today, people of Maori descent live in New Zealand's towns and cities. But they still keep alive the art, language and dances of their ancestors.

31

INDEX OF PLACE NAMES

Published in the United States, Canada, and Puerto Rico
by Hammond World Atlas Corporation
Union, New Jersey 07083
www.hammondmap.com

Copyright © 2001 Orpheus Books Ltd

Created and produced by Nicholas Harris, Joanna
Turner and Claire Aston, Orpheus Books Ltd

Illustrators Gary Hincks, Nicki Palin

ISBN 0-8437-1467-0

Library of Congress Card Number: 00-109282

Printed and bound in Belgium.

ABBREVIATIONS USED IN THIS ATLAS

Br.	(Great) Britain
Fr.	France
I.	Island
Is.	Islands
L.	Lake
Mts.	Mountains
Pr.	Prince
US	United States